KID PALEONTOLOGIST

EXPLORE THE REMARKABLE DINOSAURS, FOSSILS FINDS, AND DISCOVERIES OF THE PREHISTORIC ERA

Travel Back in Time and Meet the Most
Fascinating Creatures in History

Illustrated by Julius Csotonyi

APPLESAUCE PRESS

TABLE *OF* CONTENTS

INTRODUCTION

You've probably heard of dinosaurs, but do you know about the scientists who study them? Paleontologists are specialized scientists who study fossils to learn about the history of life on Earth. The term "fossils" can mean a few different things. Some fossils are preserved pieces of animal bodies (e.g., bones, shells, teeth, and other hard body parts). A fossil can also be the preserved imprint of an animal body in rock. Another type of fossil is a trace fossil, which is a mark from an animal like a track or trail (e.g., footprints), a burrow, or feeding and resting marks. Studying fossils allows paleontologists to figure out how old the rocks around them are, teaching us about the timeline of life on our planet.

Paleontologists don't just study dinosaurs—they study all fossils. That means they study all kinds of animals, plants, and even people from the past. There are prehistoric mammals and sea creatures that are ancestors to a lot of the animals you see around you today, but undoubtedly one of the most interesting creatures that paleontologists study is the dinosaur.

Dinosaurs (Dinosauria) were a group of prehistoric reptiles that came in all shapes and sizes. They're part of a bigger group of animals called archosaurs, which includes pterosaurs (another extinct group), birds, and crocodylians. Dinosaurs are fascinating to learn about, and paleontologists are the ones who gather and share information about them.

Because most dinosaurs went extinct millions of years ago, the only trace of them that remains is fossil evidence.

Fossils must be carefully removed from the rock surrounding them.

Studying fossils helps paleontologists to learn about the anatomy of different animals, but it also helps them to learn about their behaviors, environments, and interactions. Fossils can show whether an animal was an herbivore (plant eater) or a carnivore (meat eater). Fossil locations can help us to understand whether an animal lived alone or in a herd. And fossils can even tell us how an animal would have moved—whether it was a slow or fast runner, whether it walked on two feet (bipedal) or four (quadrupedal), or whether it could fly or glide.

Without paleontologists, we wouldn't be able to uncover all of the connections between modern and ancient life. Those connections are crucial for helping us to better understand the present and better anticipate the future.

PALEONTOLOGY 101

The field of paleontology took off in the late 1800s—that's when they first began to identify dinosaur bones. The field of paleontology has adapted and grown as more fossils have been discovered and as scientific studies have advanced.

Paleontologists study for years to become experts in their field. Someone in a paleontological career will need to understand lots of different types of sciences, from biology and chemistry to geology, archaeology, and anthropology. They take all kinds of science and math courses in school, and they usually study some kind of life science in college (like biology). After they get an undergraduate degree, they go on to get a master's degree, or even a doctorate, in paleontology.

Paleontology jobs can be in universities, museums, companies, or federal government agencies. It can involve preparation work, like planning and directing projects; fieldwork, like finding and collecting fossil samples; and preservation work, like cleaning and transporting fossil finds. But working on fossil dig projects isn't the only work paleontologists do. They also do a lot of research work in laboratories analyzing and studying what they find. And a lot of paleontologists will share their findings by writing journal articles or teaching college courses.

WITHIN THE FIELD OF PALEONTOLOGY, THERE ARE DIFFERENT SPECIALTY AREAS:

- Micropaleontologists study microscopic fossils.
- Paleobotanists study plant fossils.
- Palynologists study pollen and spores.
- Invertebrate paleontologists study fossils of invertebrate animals.
- Vertebrate paleontologists study fossils of vertebrate animals.
- Ichnologists study fossil tracks and trails.
- Paleoecologists study ecologists and climates.
- Taphonomists study fossil creation.
- Paleoanthropologists study prehistoric humans.

So how can you be a paleontologist as a kid? Consider doing your next science fair project on paleontology. Look into whether local museums, colleges, or libraries have any fossil-related activities or excursions (or simply head to a museum to take a look at pieces of the past). Check out your yard or neighborhood and see if you can find any fossil evidence in the wild. You might have to wait until you're an adult to become a certified paleontologist, but you can start to love learning right now!

PALEONTOLOGIST MEET-AND-GREET: 10 FAMOUS PALEONTOLOGISTS

Mary Anning: Mary Anning was a pioneer in paleontology. At a time when women weren't allowed to be involved in sciences, Anning was scouring England for fossils. She sold fossil mollusks and invertebrates to locals, and she uncovered remains of marine reptiles and pterosaurs (the first pterosaur fossils discovered outside of Germany). Some people think she was the inspiration for the tongue twister "She sells seashells by the seashore." Anning died in 1847.

Edward Drinker Cope: Edward Drinker Cope was best known for his part in the "Bone Wars" of the late 1800s. His rivalry with Othniel C. Marsh led the two on a competitive race to discover the most fossils. During his career, Cope wrote over 600 papers and gave names to more than 1,000 fossil species (including dozens of fish and dinosaurs). Cope died in 1897.

Othniel C. Marsh: The other half of the "Bone Wars" rivalry, Othniel C. Marsh named some of the most famous dinosaurs around (including *Allosaurus*, *Stegosaurus*, and *Triceratops*). Not only did he discover dozens of new species, but his theories on the origins of birds paved the way for a better understanding of dinosaur evolution. Marsh died in 1899.

Barnum Brown: Chief fossil hunter of New York's American Museum of Natural History, Barnum Brown was known for speeding up his expeditions by using dynamite. He discovered fossils of many different animals, but one of his most important discoveries was the first documented remains of *Tyrannosaurus*. Brown died in 1963.

Luis Alvarez: Nobel Prize–winning physicist Luis Alvarez was the first scientist to theorize that an asteroid impact was what killed the dinosaurs 65 million years ago. The theory is now called the "Alvarez Hypothesis." He discovered evidence of an impact crater in Mexico on an expedition with his son, Walter, that supported the theory. Alvarez died in 1988.

Edwin "Ned" Colbert: Ned Colbert's discoveries pioneered one of the most important theories in the study of ancient life: continental drift. His field work led to the discovery of fossils from the same species of animal in both Antarctica and South Africa. This told scientists that the two continents were once connected in a giant landmass, and helped them to better understand dinosaur evolution. Colbert died in 2001.

John Ostrom: In the 1960s, John Ostrom revolutionized the field of paleontology. He theorized that dinosaurs were more closely related to nonflying birds than they were to lizards (as paleontologists previously thought), and his studies proved that modern birds are descendants of dinosaurs. His studies also improved paleontologists' understanding of how dinosaurs (particularly hadrosaurs) stood and moved. He discovered the dinosaur *Deinonychus*, and he suggested that some dinosaurs were warm-blooded. Ostrom died in 2005.

Zofia Kielan-Jaworowska: Polish paleontologist Zofia Kielan-Jaworowska led several incredibly successful fossil expeditions in the Gobi Desert in the 1960s. Her finds included dinosaurs and ancient mammals, and one estimate said that her team discovered over 20 tons of fossils. She was a researcher and professor, and she authored the book *Hunting for Dinosaurs*. Kielan-Jaworowska died in 2015.

Dong Zhiming: A pioneer of paleontology in China, Dong Zhiming has made incredible progress in studying the Middle Jurassic Period. Zhiming has uncovered remains from dozens of dinosaurs, including hadrosaurs and sauropods. His discoveries at the bone beds in Dashanpu, Zigong, have been crucial in the understanding of dinosaur evolution. Zhiming is retired.

John "Jack" Horner: Jack Horner is one of the best-known paleontologists in the United States. His discovery of a *Maiasaura* nesting site revealed how dinosaurs built nests and cared for their young, and he discovered an enormous collection of *Tyrannosaurus* specimens and hypothesized that *T. rex* was a scavenger dinosaur. Horner was one of the inspirations for the character Dr. Alan Grant in *Jurassic Park*, and he even served as an advisor for the movies. Horner is the author of *How to Build a Dinosaur*, and he is currently studying dinosaur DNA.

DINOS AROUND THE WORLD: 10 FAMOUS FOSSIL SITES

The Anacleto Formation, Argentina: This site, dating from the Late Cretaceous Period, contained nests of fossilized eggs, including eggs and bones from titanosaurs.

The Hell Creek Formation, United States: This enormous site from the Late Cretaceous Period spans Montana, Wyoming, and North and South Dakota. Fossils from some of the most famous dinosaurs, including *Ankylosaurus*, *Triceratops*, and *Tyrannosaurus*, have been discovered there.

The Jurassic Coast, England: This Jurassic Period World Heritage site (designated by UNESCO) runs along 95 miles (152 kilometers) of coastline and is a popular fossil-hunting spot that has yielded fossils of mollusks, fish, and dinosaurs.

The Morrison Formation, United States: This massive formation stretches all the way from North Dakota to Arizona (it's named for Morrison, Colorado). It was one of the main sites of the "Bone Wars," and it held fossils of *Stegosaurus*, *Allosaurus*, and *Brachiosaurus*.

Dinosaur Provincial Park, Canada: Fossils from hundreds of dinosaur species have been found at this formation, including fossils of ceratopsians and hadrosaurs. It dates back to the Late Cretaceous Period.

Dashanpu Formation, China: A gas company crew unearthed a theropod fossil at this site while they were working, and paleontologists quickly learned that the area was rich with fossil evidence (including dinosaurs, turtles, pterosaurs, and prehistoric crocodiles) from the Late Jurassic Period.

Dinosaur Cove, Australia: During the Middle Cretaceous Period, this Australian site would have been very close to Antarctica. The fossils found there have been important for understanding how dinosaurs like *Leallynasaura* adapted to cold, dark climates.

The Solnhofen Limestone Beds, Germany: The discovery of *Archaeopteryx*, the first dinosaur found with feathers, at this site was a huge advancement in the theory of evolution.

The Flaming Cliffs, Mongolia: This remote desert site yielded some of the most famous dinosaur finds—*Velociraptor*, *Oviraptor*, and *Protoceratops*. The discovery of eggs at this site proved that dinosaurs laid eggs rather than giving birth to live young.

The Baharija Formation, Egypt: Rich in plant and aquatic animal fossils, this site at the base of an oil reservoir was also the home to several sauropods and theropods, including the *Spinosaurus*.

PREHISTORIC TIMELINE

Dinosaurs walked the Earth for millions of years, from the Triassic Period (about 225 million years ago) until the end of the Cretaceous period (about 65 million years ago). Some species of dinosaurs went extinct naturally as time passed. Extinction can happen for different reasons, and changing environments and competition for food sources are often the culprits. But at the end of the Cretaceous Period, a mass extinction event wiped out most of the remaining dinosaurs. Some scientists think that gradual climate change or volcanic eruptions were to blame, but one of the most common theories is that an asteroid impact triggered the extinction event.

PERMIAN PERIOD

299 TO 252 MILLION YEARS AGO

TRIASSIC PERIOD

252 TO 201 MILLION YEARS AGO

JURASSIC PERIOD

201 TO 145 MILLION YEARS AGO

CRETACEOUS PERIOD

145 TO 66 MILLION YEARS AGO

CENOZOIC ERA

66 MILLION YEARS AGO TO PRESENT DAY

DINOSAUR CLASSIFICATION

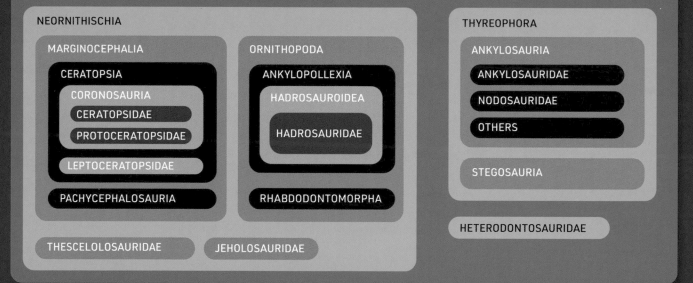

ORNITHISCHIA

NEORNITHISCHIA

MARGINOCEPHALIA

CERATOPSIA

CORONOSAURIA

CERATOPSIDAE

PROTOCERATOPSIDAE

LEPTOCERATOPSIDAE

PACHYCEPHALOSAURIA

ORNITHOPODA

ANKYLOPOLLEXIA

HADROSAUROIDEA

HADROSAURIDAE

RHABDODONTOMORPHA

THYREOPHORA

ANKYLOSAURIA

ANKYLOSAURIDAE

NODOSAURIDAE

OTHERS

STEGOSAURIA

HETERODONTOSAURIDAE

THESCELOLOSAURIDAE   JEHOLOSAURIDAE

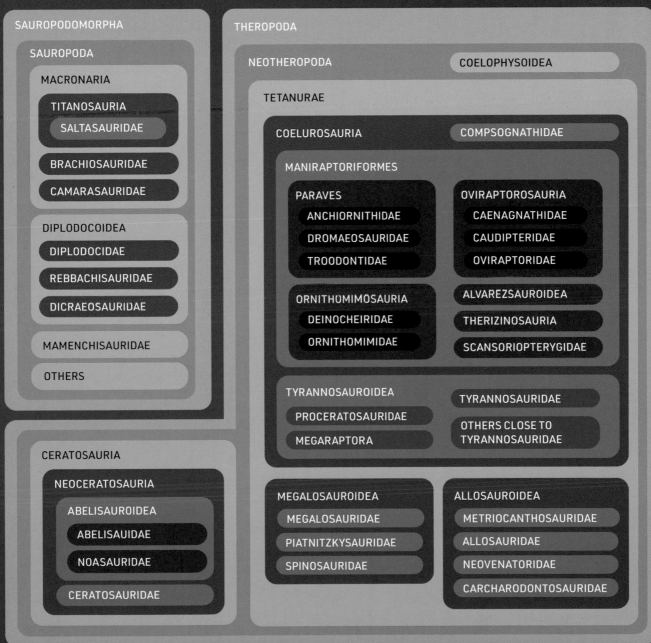

SAURISCHIA (INCLUDING EARLY SAURISCIANS)

SAUROPODOMORPHA

SAUROPODA

MACRONARIA

TITANOSAURIA
SALTASAURIDAE

BRACHIOSAURIDAE

CAMARASAURIDAE

DIPLODOCOIDEA

DIPLODOCIDAE

REBBACHISAURIDAE

DICRAEOSAURIDAE

MAMENCHISAURIDAE

OTHERS

CERATOSAURIA

NEOCERATOSAURIA

ABELISAUROIDEA

ABELISAUIDAE

NOASAURIDAE

CERATOSAURIDAE

THEROPODA

NEOTHEROPODA   COELOPHYSOIDEA

TETANURAE

COELUROSAURIA   COMPSOGNATHIDAE

MANIRAPTORIFORMES

PARAVES
ANCHIORNITHIDAE
DROMAEOSAURIDAE
TROODONTIDAE

ORNITHOMIMOSAURIA
DEINOCHEIRIDAE
ORNITHOMIMIDAE

OVIRAPTOROSAURIA
CAENAGNATHIDAE
CAUDIPTERIDAE
OVIRAPTORIDAE

ALVAREZSAUROIDEA

THERIZINOSAURIA

SCANSORIOPTERYGIDAE

TYRANNOSAUROIDEA

PROCERATOSAURIDAE

MEGARAPTORA

TYRANNOSAURIDAE

OTHERS CLOSE TO
TYRANNOSAURIDAE

MEGALOSAUROIDEA

MEGALOSAURIDAE

PIATNITZKYSAURIDAE

SPINOSAURIDAE

ALLOSAUROIDEA

METRIOCANTHOSAURIDAE

ALLOSAURIDAE

NEOVENATORIDAE

CARCHARODONTOSAURIDAE

DINOSAURIA

Not all prehistoric creatures were dinosaurs, but they were certainly among the most beloved. The name Dinosauria means "terrible lizard," and although dinosaurs might resemble lizards, they're not closely related. Dinosaurs were reptiles (like lizards), but their legs were straight underneath their hips. Lizards and crocodiles have sprawling legs that give them their distinctive crawl-like walk. Lizards likely split from the dinosaur family (and the overall archosaur group) about 270 million years ago.

There are two key groups within Dinosauria. They are called Saurischia ("lizard hips") and Ornithschia ("bird hips"). Saurischia is separated into Sauropodomorpha and Theropoda, and Ornithischia is separated into Thyreophora and Neornithischia. But not all dinosaurs fit neatly into one of these groups, and in this section we'll learn about some of the dinosaurs that defy classification.

TAWA

Fossils of *Tawa* were found along with other carnivorous dinosaurs at a site called Hayden Quarry. This site in New Mexico is estimated to be 215 to 213 million years old. *Tawa* has a mix of features that lines up with different groups of dinosaurs, which makes it hard to determine exactly what *Tawa* was. Recent analysis has found that *Tawa* should be classified as a possible early saurischian, separate from Sauropodomorpha and Theropoda.

NAME MEANING: Named after the Puebloan sun god
ERA IT LIVED IN: Late Triassic Period of North America
SIZE: Up to 8 feet (2.4 meters) long and 33 pounds (15 kilograms)
DIET: Carnivorous

EOCURSOR

Paleontologists spent years studying *Eocursor*. Fossils were first found in 1993, but the species wasn't defined until nearly 15 years later, in 2007. Paleontologists have a pretty complete skeleton of *Eocursor*, including parts of the skull, a complete set of arm and leg bones, and neck, back, and tail vertebrae. Dinosaur family trees can be incredibly complex, but *Eocursor* was most likely an ancestor to dinosaurs like stegosaurs, ceratopsians, and hadrosaurids in the Ornithischia group.

NAME MEANING: Dawn runner
ERA IT LIVED IN: Late Jurassic Period of Africa
SIZE: 3 feet (0.9 meters) long
DIET: Herbivorous

HERRERASAURUS

You don't have to be a paleontologist to discover fossils. The first fossils of *Herrerasaurus* were found by accident by a goat herder in Argentina named Victorino Herrera. Since they were still evolving, early dinosaurs didn't always fall neatly into groups. *Herrerasaurus* is an outlier dinosaur. It didn't quite fit into either the sauropodomorph or theropod groups, and instead it branched into its own family, the Herrerasauridae.

Paleontologists can tell it was carnivorous because it had dozens of serrated teeth. *Herrerasaurus* had strong back legs that would have made this bipedal dinosaur a fast runner. Each of its feet had five toes, but paleontologists think that only the three middle toes were useful in bearing this dinosaur's weight, and its long, thick tail would have also been used to help it balance.

NAME MEANING: Victorino Herrera's lizard
ERA IT LIVED IN: Late Triassic Period of South America
SIZE: Up to 20 feet (6.1 meters) long and 1,760 pounds (798.3 kilograms)
DIET: Carnivorous

HETERODONTOSAURUS

Paleontologists study dinosaur teeth to understand what they ate. Tooth shape and size can reveal a lot about diet. *Heterodontosaurus*'s teeth were different shapes and sizes (called heterodontid teeth); it had two pairs of tusks and leaf-shaped, serrated back teeth. The tooth shape and combination tell paleontologists that *Heterodontosaurus* probably ate tougher vegetation like seeds and roots, and it may have even been omnivorous. Having this kind of diet would have helped to lessen competition with other herbivore dinosaurs like sauropodomorphs. The longer-necked dinosaurs could eat vegetation that was higher up, while *Heterodontosaurus* stayed closer to the ground to search for food. *Heterodontosaurus* even had muscly arms that would have been great for digging. *Heterodontosaurus* was an ornithischian dinosaur, but it didn't belong to Neornithischia or Thyreophora; instead, it is placed within Heterodontosauridae.

NAME MEANING: Different tooth lizard

ERA IT LIVED IN: Early Jurassic Period of Africa

SIZE: 3 feet (0.9 meters) long and up to 7 pounds (3.2 kilograms)

DIET: Either herbivorous or omnivorous

KULINDADROMEUS

Fossils aren't just bones. Sometimes, they can reveal what kind of skin a dinosaur had. Studying *Kulindadromeus* showed paleontologists a layer that covered its skin called integument, which would have been a hairlike fuzz. That fuzz wasn't the only thing *Kulindadromeus* had. Fossils of its tail, hands, ankles, and feet also showed that it had scales on its body.

NAME MEANING: Kulinda site runner
ERA IT LIVED IN: Middle Jurassic Period of Asia
SIZE: 1.5 feet (0.5 meters) long
DIET: Herbivorous

CHILESAURUS

Chilesaurus had features from a bunch of different dinosaur groups, which made it really tough for paleontologists to figure out where it fit. It had birdlike hips like ornithischians, a body like theropods, and feet like sauropodomorphs. Instead of putting it into one of these groups, paleontologists consider to be part of the wider dinosauromorph grouping.

NAME MEANING: Chile lizard
ERA IT LIVED IN: Late Jurassic Period of South America
SIZE: Up to 10 feet (3 meters) long
DIET: Herbivorous

THESCELOSAURUS

Paleontologists never quite know what they'll find when they study new fossils, and a *Thescelosaurus* specimen nicknamed "Willo" presented a puzzle. It had a preserved structure in its chest that they thought might be a heart. When they studied the fossil to learn what it was, they discovered that it wasn't a heart at all—it was a mass of minerals called a concretion.

NAME MEANING: Marvelous lizard
ERA IT LIVED IN: Late Cretaceous Period of North America
SIZE: Up to 13.1 feet (4 meters) long and 600 pounds (272.2 kilograms). A larger specimen may have reached a length of 14.8 feet (4.5 meters).
DIET: Herbivorous

LEAELLYNASAURA

Dinosaur fossils have been found on just about every continent—these amazing creatures could even survive in polar climates. Fossils of *Leaellynasaura* have been found in Australia, and it would have lived near the Antarctic Circle, where it endured long, dark winter nights. *Leaellynasaura* well-adapted for its region with a fuzzy coating to keep warm and large eyes that helped it to see in the dimly lit environment.

NAME MEANING: Leaellyn Rich's lizard
ERA IT LIVED IN: Early Cretaceous Period of Australia
SIZE: 3 feet (0.9 meters) long
DIET: Herbivorous

ORODROMEUS

Even dinosaurs took care of their young. At least, that's what paleontologist Jack Horner believes. Horner named *Orodromeus*, which was discovered along with a nest filled with its eggs at a site called Egg Mountain, found in Montana in the United States.

NAME MEANING: Mountain runner
ERA IT LIVED IN: Late Cretaceous Period of North America
SIZE: 8.2 feet (2.5 meters) long and 22 pounds (10 kilograms)
DIET: Herbivorous

ORYCTODROMEUS

Oryctodromeus helped paleontologists to learn more about different dinosaur behaviors and survival methods. *Oryctodromeus* was a burrower, and paleontologists were able to study fossils of one adult and two young *Oryctodromeus* preserved in a burrow. Paleontologists think that *Oryctodromeus* may have lived in burrows and taken care of its young there.

NAME MEANING: Digging runner
ERA IT LIVED IN: Late Cretaceous Period of North America
SIZE: Up to 6.9 feet (2.1 meters) long and 71 pounds (32.2 kilograms)
DIET: Herbivorous

SAUROPODOMORPHA

Sauropodomorpha were herbivorous dinosaurs with leaf-shaped teeth, a small head, and iconic long necks. Their necks had 10 or more vertebrae, were longer than their limbs, and were at least as long as the trunk of their body. Sauropodomorpha fossils have been found from the Triassic, Jurassic, and Cretaceous Periods, but they were most abundant during the Triassic.

An early group of Sauropodomorpha were bipedal dinosaurs (walking on two legs) called prosauropods. The more well-known dinos of this family were a later group called the sauropods, quadrupedal (walking on four legs) dinosaurs with four pillar-like legs.

EORAPTOR

Eoraptor looks a lot more like a theropod than a sauropodomorph physically, but paleontologists were able to use evidence from *Eoraptor* bones to determine that it was indeed a sauropodomorph despite its small head, short arms, and long legs. Those legs, paired with a small body, would have made *Eoraptor* a fast-running dinosaur that could dodge predators. Fossils have been found in Argentina and Madagascar, including skulls and three complete *Eoraptor* skeletons. The skulls paleontologists have studied weren't fused and had eye sockets that were very large compared to the rest of the skull. These two traits are common in young skulls, which has led paleontologists to think that they may not have found any adult remains yet.

Eoraptor had short, grasping hands with five fingers, which it could use to grab onto prey. Although it had five fingers, paleontologists suspect that only about three of them were really effective for grabbing. The other two stubby fingers weren't very useful, which might explain why later species of dinosaurs had fewer fingers.

NAME MEANING: Dawn thief
ERA IT LIVED IN: Late Triassic Period of South America
SIZE: 3 feet (0.9 meters) long and 22 pounds (10 kilograms)
DIET: Omnivorous

PLATEOSAURUS

Paleontologists don't just study what dinosaurs looked like and ate; they also study how they moved. Most land-based animals are either bipedal or quadrupedal, meaning they either walk on two legs (think: humans) or on four legs (think: dogs and cats). A lot of sauropodomorphs were quadrupedal, and at first paleontologists thought *Plateosaurus* was too. But after doing more research, they learned that *Plateosaurus* couldn't rotate its hands, and its arms may not have been strong enough to support its weight. So instead of walking on all fours like other sauropodomorphs, *Plateosaurus* was probably bipedal.

Fossils of *Plateosaurus* have been found in more than 50 different locations across north and central Europe and Greenland. In one dig location in Germany, paleontologists found nearly complete skeletons of 35 different *Plateosaurus* as well as pieces of remains from dozens more. Finding lots of dinosaurs in one place could mean that *Plateosaurus* lived in herds.

CETIOSAURUS

Dinosaurs weren't the only creatures roaming the Earth in prehistoric times, and paleontologists spend plenty of time studying fossils of other types of animals that lived on land, in the air, and under the water. Crocodylians, the prehistoric ancestor of modern crocodiles, lived in a lot of the same environments as dinosaurs, but they spent most of their time in or near water (just like crocodiles). When *Cetiosaurus* was first discovered, paleontologists thought that this dinosaur was a crocodylian based on its bones. But once they studied it more, they realized it was a land animal, not a marine animal like crocodylians, and they were able to identify it as a sauropod.

NAME MEANING: Whale lizard
ERA IT LIVED IN: Middle Jurassic Period of Europe
SIZE: Up to 52 feet (15.8 meters) long and 11 tons (10 metric tons)
DIET: Herbivorous

MUSSAURUS

When paleontologists first discovered *Mussaurus*, they thought it was a tiny dino—that's why they named it "mouse lizard." But later they discovered new *Mussaurus* skeletons and realized it wasn't so small. The first ones they studied were just infants and juveniles. Once they were able to compare those first fossils with the adults, they were able to learn a lot about how this dinosaur changed as it grew. Their skulls and necks lengthened as they got older, and paleontologists think they may have even transitioned from being quadrupedal to bipedal as they grew up, kind of like how human babies go from crawling to walking.

NAME MEANING: Mouse lizard
ERA IT LIVED IN: Early Jurassic Period of South America
SIZE: Up to 20 feet (6.1 meters) long and 2,200 pounds (998 kilograms)
DIET: Herbivorous

CAMARASAURUS

Paleontologists put similar dinosaurs together in groups, each of which is called a genus. The *Camarasaurus* genus has four different species in it: *Camarasaurus grandis*, *Camarasaurus lentus*, *Camarasaurus lewisi*, and *Camarasaurus supremus*. All of the *Camarasaurus* species were quite large at around 49 feet (14.9 meters) long, but *Camarasaurus supremus* was the largest of them all at 75 feet (22.9 meters) long. The shape of *Camarasaurus* teeth tells paleontologists a lot about what they ate. The teeth were chisel shaped, which would have been best for eating rough plant material.

Camarasaurus had front legs that were shorter than its hind legs, like most sauropods, but it also had an interesting body shape, where its shoulder blades were low and its hips were high. This would have allowed its legs to somewhat line up even though they weren't the same length.

NAME MEANING: Chambered lizard
ERA IT LIVED IN: Late Jurassic Period of North America
SIZE: About 49 feet (14.9 meters) long. Larger specimens may have grown up to 75 feet (22.9 meters) long.
DIET: Herbivorous

DIPLODOCUS

Modern depictions of dinosaurs like you see in movies and tv shows often stick to a few standard dinosaur "shapes." You can probably pretty easily identify a tyrannosaur that stands up on its hind legs or a ceratosaur with its horned and frilled face based on dino images you've seen. *Diplodocus* is probably what you think of most when you picture sauropod dinosaurs. They have a classic sauropod body shape with a long neck and tail and pillar-like legs. It's the most identifiable sauropod, and that's probably because paleontologists have a lot of fossils to study. Fossils of many different species have been found at the Morrison Formation in North America, but *Diplodocus* was one of the most common. More fossils means more knowledge, and paleontologists have been able to learn a lot about *Diplodocus* and how it grew and lived. Young *Diplodocus* would eat lots of different types of vegetation, but as they got older they would grow rapidly (kind of like how lots of kids go through a growth spurt) and they would get a little pickier about what type of food they ate.

Not all museums can display real fossils, so sometimes they will make plaster recreations called casts to put on display. One *Diplodocus* cast, fondly known as Dippy, made this dinosaur famous in museums. When Dippy was first displayed, it had its tail down low to the ground. But, when paleontologists learned that the tail was likely raised for balance, museum curators at the Natural History Museum in London realized they would need to adjust the cast on display. By 1993 the tail was raised to accurately reflect its position, balancing out the neck.

NAME MEANING: Double beam
ERA IT LIVED IN: Late Jurassic Period of North America
SIZE: Up to 85 feet (25.9 meters) long and 16.3 tons (14.8 metric tons). Larger specimens may have grown up to 105 feet (32 meters) long.
DIET: Herbivorous

APATOSAURUS

Sometimes, paleontologists are lucky enough to find complete skeleton fossils, but sometimes they only uncover pieces. That's exactly what happened with *Apatosaurus*. When it was first discovered, it was missing its skull, and paleontologists had to guess what it would have looked like. Initially, they guessed that *Apatosaurus* had a skull like *Camarasaurus*. Luckily, they eventually found an *Apatosaurus* skull, but when they did they realized that it looked more like the skull of *Diplodocus* than *Camarasaurus*.

One of the biggest debates about *Apatosaurus* and other sauropods is over how flexible their necks were. While paleontologists once thought that their necks were stiff, comparison to modern animals like swans shows that they may have had flexible, S-shaped necks.

Fossils of *Apatosaurus* were first found near riverbanks, and their unusually shaped bones look similar to the bones of aquatic animals. Paleontologists once thought that they may have been able to swim or live in the water, but newer research shows that they probably stayed on land and ate ferns, plants, and algae.

NAME MEANING: Deceptive lizard
ERA IT LIVED IN: Late Jurassic Period of North America
SIZE: Up to 75 feet (22.9 meters) long and 22.4 tons (20.3 metric tons)
DIET: Herbivorous

BRONTOSAURUS

Dinosaur species and groupings change as paleontologists discover more fossils and learn more about each. Sometimes what they thought was one species turns out to be entirely different. *Brontosaurus* and *Apatosaurus* were thought to be the same species until a 2015 study proved they were different from each other.

NAME MEANING: Thunder lizard
ERA IT LIVED IN: Late Jurassic Period of North America
SIZE: Up to 72 feet (21.9 meters) long and 15 tons (13.6 metric tons)
DIET: Herbivorous

BRACHIOSAURUS

Don't believe everything you see on screen. Jurassic Park shows a *Brachiosaurus* rearing up on its hind legs, but paleontologists doubt that would have been possible. *Brachiosaurus* had very long front legs, and its tail and short back legs probably wouldn't have been able to support the weight of the dinosaur if it had reared up. Those legs differed from other sauropod species that had front legs that were shorter than the back, which caused them to lean slightly forward. Because of its longer front legs, *Brachiosaurus* would have been tipped slightly upward when standing.

NAME MEANING: Arm lizard
ERA IT LIVED IN: Late Jurassic Period of North America
SIZE: Up to 69 feet (21 meters) long and 50 tons (45.4 metric tons)
DIET: Herbivorous

RAPETOSAURUS

Most sauropod dinosaurs lived alongside other herbivore dinosaurs (ornithopods, thyreophorans, and ceratopsians, for example). *Rapetosaurus* fossils were found in Madagascar and showed that it lived in an unusual environment—it was the only known large herbivore in its habitat. But it wasn't the only dinosaur in the area. The *Majungasaurus*, a carnivorous dinosaur, was also found in Madagascar, and may have hunted *Rapetosaurus*. Paleontologists have noticed bite marks on *Rapetosaurus* bones that they think would have been caused by *Majungasaurus*.

NAME MEANING: Rapeto lizard
ERA IT LIVED IN: Late Cretaceous Period of Africa
SIZE: Up to 54 feet (16.5 meters) long and 11.3 tons (10.3 metric tons)
DIET: Herbivorous

NIGERSAURUS

You might not expect herbivores to have a ton of teeth, but *Nigersaurus* proves that any kind of dinosaur can have a mouth full. *Nigersaurus* had a skull shaped like a vacuum cleaner and a wide mouth filled with a whopping 500 teeth. It didn't use those teeth to hunt other animals; instead, it would have fed on vegetation like ferns, horsetails, and flowering plants near where it lived on riverbanks or in wetlands. The downward-positioned snout would have helped it to reach those low-lying plants.

SAUROPOSEIDON

One type of fossil, called petrified wood, is created when ancient wood slowly turns to stone. The fossils of *Sauroposeidon* were so unusual that when they were first discovered in 1994 paleontologists thought they might be petrified wood instead of bones from a real creature.

Paleontologists can estimate how tall different sauropods were by studying their long necks, which is how they estimated that *Sauroposeidon* may have been one of the tallest sauropods around. Neck vertebrae are the only fossils paleontologists have found of *Sauroposeidon*, but they immediately noticed that the vertebrae were incredibly long. One vertebrae measured 4.6 feet (1.4 meters) long! Most sauropods had 11 to 19 neck vertebrae, so paleontologists estimated that *Sauroposeidon* could have grown to be 69 feet (21 meters) tall. *Brachiosaurus*, in comparison, would have been around 43 feet (13.1 meters) tall.

NAME MEANING: Lizard earthquake god
ERA IT LIVED IN: Early Cretaceous Period of North America
SIZE: Up to 112 feet (34.1 meters) long and 60 tons (54.4 metric tons)
DIET: Herbivorous

ARGENTINOSAURUS

NAME MEANING: Argentina lizard
ERA IT LIVED IN: Late Cretaceous Period of South America
SIZE: Up to 115 feet (35.1 meters) long and 82.6 tons (74.9 metric tons)
DIET: Herbivorous

Fossils of *Argentinosaurus* were found at the Huincul Formation in Argentina alongside evidence of non-dinosaurian animals such as turtles, crocodylians, fish, and lizards. By studying the geology of the discovery site, paleontologists were able to discover what kind of environment *Argentinosaurus* would have lived in. They learned that *Argentinosaurus* lived in a forested environment that would have had rivers, streams, and different types of plants like conifers and ferns.

ALAMOSAURUS

Just like groups of people, groups of dinosaurs migrated from one place to another over time. Studying the links between different species helps paleontologists to understand where they started and where they moved to. The first fossils of *Alamosaurus* were found in southern North America, and this discovery was pretty surprising to paleontologists because there weren't any other sauropod fossils in North America during the Late Cretaceous Period. Paleontologists studying *Alamosaurus* have tried to understand where its ancestors came from. Some paleontologists think *Alamosaurus* ancestors would have migrated to North America from Asia, but others think it's more likely that their ancestors started out in South America.

NAME MEANING: Ojo Alamo lizard
ERA IT LIVED IN: Late Cretaceous Period of North America
SIZE: Up to 85.3 feet (26 meters) long and 41.8 tons (37.9 metric tons)
DIET: Herbivorous

SALTASAURUS

Fossils of *Saltasaurus* show evidence of a type of bony armor called osteoderms, which opened up a lot of questions about the sauropod group called titanosaurs. If *Saltasaurus* had osteoderms, paleontologists wonder whether other titanosaurs might have had them as well. The osteoderms were likely a defense against predators. Paleontologists think that unidentified titanosaur eggs containing unborn babies displaying dermal armor, found in a fossilized nesting site in Argentina, may have been baby *Saltasaurus*.

NAME MEANING: Salta lizard

ERA IT LIVED IN: Late Cretaceous Period of South America

SIZE: Up to 42 feet (12.8 meters) long and 7.6 tons (6.9 metric tons)

DIET: Herbivorous

THEROPODA

The Theropoda dinosaurs, called theropods, had hollow bones and claws on each limb. Most theropods had three toes and were carnivores, but some adapted differently and became omnivores. Coelurosauria was a group of feathered theropods that includes a lot of dinosaurs you might know, like tyrannosaurs and raptors. The feathers weren't always all over their bodies—sometimes they had just a few feathers on their legs and sometimes the feathers were what paleontologists call protofeathers, with a branched structure similar to bird feathers.

In the Jurassic Period, birds evolved from the coelurosaurian dinosaurs into a small subgroup called Avialae. These prehistoric birds developed wings and took flight, and they were the only group of dinosaurs to survive mass extinction. That means modern birds are the only living relatives of dinosaurs!

DILOPHOSAURUS

Those small arms may not look formidable, but paleontologists have conducted biomechanical studies to see what *Dilophosaurus* was capable of. Not only did it have a good range of motion, *Dilophosaurus* could also grasp with its clawed fingers, which would have been incredibly helpful in catching prey. *Dilophosaurus* was an apex predator, which means it was at the top of the food chain in its environment. Theatrical depictions of *Dilophosaurus* show it with a huge collared frill spewing venom, but that's just for the screen. *Dilophosaurus* had two crests on top of its head (no frills) and, even though it was an incredible hunter, it couldn't spit venom.

At one fossil site in southern Utah, paleontologists have uncovered a spot where a *Dilophosaurus*—or very similar dinosaur—laid down for a rest. Marks in the rock called trace fossils show evidence of the dinosaur's tail, hip, feet, and hands as it sat by the side of a lake, eventually shuffling forward and walking off along the shore. This trace is the closest we can get to watching a living *Dilophosaurus*.

NAME MEANING: Double-crested lizard
ERA IT LIVED IN: Early Jurassic Period of North America
SIZE: Up to 23 feet (7 meters) long and 880 pounds (399.2 kilograms)
DIET: Carnivorous

ARCHAEOPTERYX

Archaeopteryx was a paleontological breakthrough. It was the first dinosaur fossil found with feathers, which helped paleontologists to better understand the link between dinosaurs and modern birds. Studying the fossils even showed paleontologists what color feathers *Archaeopteryx* had. It had large feathers on its feet that led paleontologists to a crucial question: could it fly? Some paleontologists think it may have been able to fly, some think it could just glide, and others think it couldn't fly at all and used its tail and wings for steering while it ran. Whether it could or couldn't fly, *Archaeopteryx* fossils were an important discovery in the understanding of birds and the origin of flight.

NAME MEANING: Ancient wing
ERA IT LIVED IN: Late Jurassic Period of Europe
SIZE: Up to 20 inches (50.8 centimeters) long and 2.2 pounds (1 kilogram)
DIET: Carnivorous

ANCHIORNIS

Like *Archaeopteryx*, *Anchiornis* fossils showed evidence of feathers. Paleontologists learned from a study in 2010 that its feathers were mostly brown, but that *Anchiornis* had red feathers on top of its head and white stripes on its wings. *Anchiornis* had feathers on both its front and back limbs, giving it four wings. Paleontologists think that the feathers and wings were large enough that *Anchiornis* would have been able to fly.

Thanks to beautifully preserved dinosaurs like *Anchiornis*, paleontologists know that birds—including every bird alive today—are descended from predatory dinosaurs. The first birds evolved about 150 million years ago, late in the Jurassic Period, and lived alongside the rest of their dinosaurian family until a mass extinction at the end of the Cretaceous Period wiped out all the non-bird dinosaurs.

NAME MEANING: Near bird
ERA IT LIVED IN: Late Jurassic Period of Asia
SIZE: Up to 1.3 feet (0.4 meters) long and 0.6 pounds (0.2 kilograms)
DIET: Carnivorous

CERATOSAURUS

Dinosaurs were land-based animals, but paleontologists think that some may have been capable of swimming. *Ceratosaurus* had a tail that may have been able to help it swim, which would have allowed it to hunt aquatic prey. Since *Ceratosaurus* was a small theropod compared to others, this adaptation would have minimized competition for food; most other theropods preyed on land animals. With its horned skull and osteoderms (bony armor) shaped like small spikes running down its body, *Ceratosaurus* looked a lot like a dragon standing on two legs.

NAME MEANING: Horn lizard

ERA IT LIVED IN: Late Jurassic Period of North America and possibly Africa and Europe

SIZE: About 18.7 feet (5.7 meters) long. Larger specimens may have reached body lengths of up to 23 feet (7 meters).

DIET: Carnivorous

ALLOSAURUS

In the late 1800s, paleontologists Edward Drinker Cope and Othniel C. Marsh got into a heated competition to discover dinosaur fossils. They fought to outdo each other on expeditions for years, and the time of their rivalry is known as the "Bone Wars." Their competitive spirits turned into a huge win for the field of paleontology; they discovered well over 100 new dinosaur species, uncovered new sites rich with fossils (called bone beds), and got the public excited to learn about prehistoric life. *Allosaurus* was just one of the many discoveries of the Bone Wars, and it was first described by Marsh after finding fossils at the Morrison Formation in North America.

One *Allosaurus* in particular, nicknamed "Big Al," has given paleontologists a lot of information about dinosaur interactions. Al had marks from multiple healed injuries on its bones, meaning that it had battled other dinosaurs and survived. The injuries could have come from attempts to prey on larger dinosaurs like *Stegosaurus* or *Diplodocus*, but some of the injuries seem to have come from combat with other *Allosaurus*.

Unlike other theropods, *Allosaurus* had flattened teeth and a weak bite force. Instead of using those teeth to crush bone (like *Tyrannosaurus*), *Allosaurus* would have been better at slicing through flesh when attacking prey. Paleontologists think that *Allosaurus* probably fed like modern falcons do, pinning carcasses with its feet and ripping off chunks of flesh with powerful jerks of its neck.

NAME MEANING: Different lizard

ERA IT LIVED IN: Late Jurassic Period of North America and Europe

SIZE: About 31.8 feet (9.7 meters) long and 2.8 tons (2.5 metric tons). Larger specimens may have reached up to 36 to 40 feet (11 to 12.2 meters) long.

DIET: Carnivorous

TYRANNOSAURUS

Tyrannosaurus (aka *T. rex*) is one of the most infamous dinosaurs around. With its large head and body, muscular tail, and tiny arms, *Tyrannosaurus* is immediately recognizable to dinosaur lovers everywhere. But although this species is one of the most well-known to the public, paleontologists actually don't have a complete skeleton of this massive dinosaur. The first *Tyrannosaurus* fossil to be discovered was located by a curator of the American Museum of Natural History, and the museum in New York City is one of the few places you can see a true *Tyrannosaurus* fossil on display.

Tyrannosaurus was a fearsome predator and, although some paleontologists think it may have been both a predator and a scavenger (meaning it both attacked prey and found food that it didn't need to hunt), it could take on enormous dinosaurs. *Tyrannosaurus* teeth were shaped like railroad spikes, and it could easily crush through bone, with a bite force of up to 15,000 pounds (6,803.9 kilograms). Paleontologists have calculated that *Tyrannosaurus* had neck muscles strong enough to throw a 110-pound chunk of meat 15 feet into the air and catch it again. Its arms may look small in comparison to the size of its body, but they could lift 400 pounds (181.4 kilograms) each. Bite marks found on bones of *Triceratops* and *Edmontosaurus* likely came from *Tyrannosaurus*.

As it grew, *T. rex* went through an enormous growth spurt: During its teen years it could pack on around 5 pounds (2.3 kilograms) per day. It reached full size around age 18, and the oldest *Tyrannosaurus* fossil analyzed was about 28 years old.

NAME MEANING: Tyrant lizard

ERA IT LIVED IN: Late Cretaceous Period of North America

SIZE: Up to 40 feet (12.2 meters) long and 9 tons (8.2 metric tons)

DIET: Carnivorous

NAME MEANING: Irritating one
ERA IT LIVED IN: Early Cretaceous Period of South America
SIZE: Up to 26 feet (7.9 meters) long and 3 tons (2.7 metric tons)
DIET: Carnivorous

IRRITATOR

The only fossil paleontologists have found of *Irritator* is its skull, but that doesn't mean they can't still learn a lot about this dinosaur. In 2020, *Irritator* was the subject of a neuroanatomy study (study of the nervous system), and preparing its skull was so frustrating for paleontologists that they gave it the name "irritating one." The study looked at *Irritator*'s inner ear and the results showed that it may have had a downward-pointing snout. This snout position is most common in dinosaurs that would have eaten aquatic animals (like *Nigersaurus*), which led paleontologists to believe it would have lived along the coast and eaten fish or other small aquatic animals. That wasn't the only thing it ate, though. Paleontologists think that a tooth found in the skeleton of a pterosaur came from *Irritator*.

BARYONYX

Baryonyx was an exciting find for paleontologists because of its skull. It had a crocodile-like snout and conical teeth, which tells paleontologists that it likely fed on fish (like modern crocodiles). It had curved claws on its hands that would have been helpful for holding onto slippery fish that *Baryonyx* caught in its coastal environment. Like *Irritator*, *Baryonyx* would have eaten other animals along with fish, and paleontologists have been able to prove this, thanks to a unique fossil. The stomach evidence of one *Baryonyx* had skeletal material from a baby *Iguanodon* inside!

NAME MEANING: Heavy claw
ERA IT LIVED IN: Early Cretaceous Period of Europe
SIZE: Up to 33 feet (10.1 meters) long and 1.9 tons (1.7 metric tons)
DIET: Carnivorous

ACROCANTHOSAURUS

One way that paleontologists can study prehistoric life is through fossilized footprints called trackways. In Texas, one trackway has footprints that belong to a theropod and a sauropod, and paleontologists suspect that they were from an *Acrocanthosaurus* hunting multiple sauropods. *Acrocanthosaurus* would have been able to use its short but powerful arms to grab prey, and paleontologists think it had an excellent sense of smell based on studies of its braincase anatomy.

Along its back, *Acrocanthosaurus* had tall spines that are a source of uncertainty for paleontologists. The spines might have just been for display, but they might have helped *Acrocanthosaurus* control its temperature. Comparisons to modern animals can sometimes shed light on prehistoric anatomy, and paleontologists think that the spines could have been attachment points for a muscular ridge, similar to a modern bison.

NAME MEANING: High-spined lizard
ERA IT LIVED IN: Early Cretaceous Period of North America
SIZE: Up to 38 feet (11.6 meters) long and 6.8 tons (6.2 metric tons)
DIET: Carnivorous

SINORNITHOSAURUS

Sinornithosaurus is a bit of a paleontological mystery. One study of its skull suggested that it might have had a venomous bite since the middle teeth in the jaw of *Sinornithosaurus* were incredibly long and fanlike, with grooves on the surface that are often found in venomous animals. Later studies debunked that theory. The shape of its teeth look a lot like those of venomous snakes, but there's no proof that *Sinornithosaurus* could produce venom.

Paleontologists also aren't sure whether the feathered *Sinornithosaurus* could fly. By studying its shoulder blade, paleontologists have learned that *Sinornithosaurus* may have been able to flap its arms like a bird. But they don't think it could truly fly; more likely, it could just glide over long distances.

NAME MEANING: Chinese bird lizard
ERA IT LIVED IN: Early Cretaceous Period of Asia
SIZE: Up to 3.9 feet (1.2 meters) long and 6.6 pounds (3 kilograms)
DIET: Carnivorous

GORGOSAURUS

Gorgosaurus fossils at different ages have allowed paleontologists to study how this dinosaur would have grown—and speculate how its behavior would have changed as it got older. When it was young, *Gorgosaurus* was lanky, and probably would have hunted prey that was about as big as it was. It wasn't until it got older that its skull and body were suited for feeding on larger prey.

Gorgosaurus had a light build and long legs that made it a very agile hunter, able to outmaneuver some of the herbivorous dinosaurs of its time. Tyrannosaurs like *Gorgosaurus* were not typically both hunters and scavengers. Thanks to its well-developed sense of smell, *Gorgosaurus* was able to sniff out rotting carcasses as well as live prey.

NAME MEANING: Dreadful lizard

ERA IT LIVED IN: Late Cretaceous
Period of North America

SIZE: Up to 30 feet (9.1 meters) long
and 3.2 tons (2.9 metric tons)

DIET: Carnivorous

QIANZHOUSAURUS

Most dinosaurs in the tyrannosaurid family had deep snouts, which is why the discovery of *Qianzhousaurus* was so exciting for paleontologists. *Qianzhousaurus* had a slender snout that would have been better suited for small prey, and the discovery proved to paleontologists that there was a group of tyrannosaurids with slender snouts. This type of group is called a clade, and paleontologists named the slender-snouted tyrannosaur clade Alioramini.

NAME MEANING: Qianzhou or Ganzhou City lizard

ERA IT LIVED IN: Late Cretaceous Period of Asia

SIZE: Up to 21 feet (6.4 meters) long and 1,669 pounds (757 kilograms)

DIET: Carnivorous

CARNOTAURUS

Carnotaurus was given the name "bull" because of the two bull-like horns over its eyes. Paleontologists have speculated that it may have used the horns for competing with other male *Carnotaurus* by headbutting. Fossils of *Carnotaurus* have skin impressions that tell paleontologists it had a rough, bumpy skin texture.

NAME MEANING: Meat-eating bull
ERA IT LIVED IN: Late Cretaceous Period of South America
SIZE: Up to 26.2 feet (8 meters) long and 1.5 tons (1.4 metric tons)
DIET: Carnivorous

SPINOSAURUS

Fossils are fragile things; even though they've survived millions of years, they aren't immune to destruction. Unfortunately, the original *Spinosaurus* fossils were destroyed in bombing during World War II. Luckily for paleontologists, more *Spinosaurus* fossils have since been uncovered.

Paleontologists have used computer-simulated studies to better understand *Spinosaurus*, with its paddle-like tail and a large sail on its back. The results have been split, with some evidence supporting the idea that *Spinosaurus* was a land-based (terrestrial) creature and other evidence indicating that *Spinosaurus* may have spent some of its time in the water (semiaquatic). Regardless of whether it lived in the water, it certainly lived near it in tidal flats and mangrove swamps, and it likely would have had a diet of both small land animals and fish.

NAME MEANING: Spine lizard
ERA IT LIVED IN: Late Cretaceous Period of Africa
SIZE: Up to 52 feet (15.8 meters) long and 7 tons (6.4 metric tons)
DIET: Carnivorous

NAME MEANING: Mahajanga Province lizard
ERA IT LIVED IN: Late Cretaceous Period of Africa
SIZE: Up to 26 feet (7.9 meters) long
DIET: Carnivorous

MAJUNGASAURUS

The *Majungasaurus* would have been an apex predator in the Late Cretaceous Period of Madagascar, and it would have taken on prey that was quite large, like the *Rapetosaurus*. Paleontologists know this because bones of *Rapetosaurus* show bite marks from *Majungasaurus*. The legs of *Majungasaurus* were short and stout, which gives paleontologists a hint as to how it hunted. It wouldn't have been very fast, so it was unlikely it pursued prey over long distances. Instead, *Majungasaurus* would have been an ambush predator that hid and waited for prey before powerfully pouncing.

BONAPARTENYKUS

Most animals don't use tools in the same way that humans do, so anything they need has to be part of their body. As different species evolve, their bodies adapt to best suit their needs. For *Bonapartenykus*, its claws were the body part that acted like a tool. *Bonapartenykus* had a large single claw on each of its short arms that paleontologists think would have been useful to dig into insect mounds and search for insects (like termites) to eat. Paired with excellent eyesight, which paleontologists believe *Bonapartenykus* had based on its skull, these pick-like claws would have been incredibly useful for hunting.

NAME MEANING: José Bonaparte's claw

ERA IT LIVED IN: Late Cretaceous Period of South America

SIZE: Up to 9.5 feet (2.9 meters) long and 75 pounds (34 kilograms)

DIET: Carnivorous

GIGANOTOSAURUS

NAME MEANING: Giant Southern lizard
ERA IT LIVED IN: Late Cretaceous Period of South America
SIZE: Up to 43 feet (13.1 meters) long and 8.8 tons (8 metric tons)
DIET: Carnivorous

Being longer doesn't always mean being heavier, and *Giganotosaurus* is a great example. Even though *Giganotosaurus* is considered the largest theropod dinosaur because of its length, it weighed less than *Tyrannosaurus* (which clocked in at a whopping 9 tons, or 8.2 metric tons). It didn't need the extra weight, though. *Giganotosaurus* had teeth that could slice flesh, and paleontologists think it fed on massive titanosaurian sauropods.

Giganotosaurus would have been pretty quick and agile. Some paleontologists think *Giganotosaurus* may have been able to run as fast as 30 miles per hour. It had a thin, pointed tail that would have been useful for balancing and making quick turns while it ran.

GALLIMIMUS

Gallimimus is part of a family of dinosaurs called ornithomimids; in fact, it's one of the best known by paleontologists since they've been able to study complete skeletons from both adults and juveniles. The ornithomimids were a group of long-legged, long-necked theropods with toothless beaks (somewhat resembling modern ostriches). By looking at *Gallimimus*, paleontologists have been able to determine that they would have been fast runners, and they may have even had feathers on their long legs.

Unlike tyrannosaurs with their massive teeth, the toothless beaks of *Gallimimus* and other ornithomimids tell paleontologists that these dinosaurs were likely omnivores. The beaks would have been useful for eating both small animals and tough vegetation. Polish paleontologist Zofia Kielan-Jaworowska, who was the first woman to lead a dinosaur expedition, speculated that *Gallimimus* may have traveled in large herds. You can see these dinosaurs depicted in a herd in the movie *Jurassic Park*.

NAME MEANING: Chicken mimic
ERA IT LIVED IN: Late Cretaceous Period of Asia
SIZE: Up to 20 feet (6.1 meters) long and 970 pounds (440 kilograms)
DIET: Omnivorous

THERIZINOSAURUS

Paleontologists have long been stumped by the massive three-foot claws on *Therizinosaurus*. When the fossils were first discovered, paleontologists thought they could have belonged to a large turtle instead of a dinosaur. Once they found more evidence of *Therizinosaurus*, they realized it was a theropod dinosaur, but they still aren't quite sure what those claws were for. Some paleontologists think they could have been used as a defense. *Therizinosaurus* lived alongside predatory tyrannosaurs, so it would have needed to be able to protect itself. But other paleontologists think that the claws may have worked more like a rake, allowing *Therizinosaurus* to rake in and grasp vegetation. If that's the case, then *Therizinosaurus* would have been either an herbivore or an omnivore.

NAME MEANING: Scythe lizard

ERA IT LIVED IN: Late Cretaceous Period of Asia

SIZE: Up to 33 feet (10.1 meters) long and 3 tons (2.7 metric tons)

DIET: Either herbivorous or omnivorous

OVIRAPTOR

Oviraptor has been given a bad reputation over the years—its name even means "egg thief"—but paleontologists now think that this dinosaur may have been misunderstood. The very first *Oviraptor* fossil discovered was of one lying on top of a nest of eggs, which led paleontologists to believe this dinosaur was stealing the eggs of another dinosaur (like a *Protoceratops*) to eat. But after studying the nest, paleontologists realized that the eggs weren't another dinosaur species at all. The nest eggs were *Oviraptor* eggs, and paleontologists started to speculate that *Oviraptor* wasn't stealing them, it was protecting them. It was probably brooding or nesting the eggs, which means it was keeping them warm and protecting them until the eggs were ready to hatch, the same way that modern birds care for their babies. *Oviraptor* shared a lot of traits with modern birds. It had a short tail, a crested head, and a toothless beak, and paleontologists think it may have had feathers.

NAME MEANING: Egg thief
ERA IT LIVED IN: Late Cretaceous Period of Asia
SIZE: Up to 5.2 feet (1.6 meters) long and 88 pounds (39.9 kilograms)
DIET: Omnivorous

DEINOCHEIRUS

Paleontologists went decades between discoveries of *Deinocheirus*. When it was first found in 1965, they only discovered a few of its bones. The discovery included a pair of unusually large arms, but paleontologists had no idea how the rest of the dinosaur looked. It wasn't until 2014 that they discovered more bones of *Deinocheirus*. This discovery included a skull, which allowed them to better analyze the dinosaur's appearance.

NAME MEANING: Terrible arms
ERA IT LIVED IN: Late Cretaceous Period of Asia
SIZE: Up to 36 feet (11 meters) long and 5.5 tons (5 metric tons)
DIET: Possibly omnivorous, feeding on both plants and small animals

NAME MEANING: Swift thief
ERA IT LIVED IN: Late Cretaceous Period of Asia
SIZE: Up to 6 feet (1.8 meters) long and 80 pounds (36.3 kilograms)
DIET: Carnivorous

VELOCIRAPTOR

Velociraptor, like *Oviraptor*, has gained a reputation over the years that it doesn't quite deserve. Modern depictions of this dinosaur have shown it as huge and incredibly intelligent, but in reality it was a fairly small dinosaur in comparison to other theropods. It may not have been a nefarious genius, but it was a skilled predator. It would have hunted smaller dinosaurs like *Oviraptor* and *Protoceratops*. One discovery of fossils in a collapsed sand dune showed a *Velociraptor* and a *Protoceratops* mid-combat.

Paleontologists think that the claw *Velociraptor* had on each foot would have been used to tackle and trap its prey. While it walked, the claw would have pointed upright. Then, when it attacked, the claw would snap downward.

THYREOPHORA

The name Thyreophora means "shield bearer," and this group
of dinosaurs had lots of protection. There are two main groups
within Thyreophora: Ankylosauria and Stegosauria.

Ankylosauria is a group of dinosaurs that had armor-like scales
protecting their bodies. They usually had spikes or horns set into
their "armor," and a lot of them had clubbed tails—they're more
commonly known as armored dinosaurs. Stegosauria dinosaurs
had more shield-like scales on their bodies in the form of large
rows of plates or spines down their backs.

SCELIDOSAURUS

One of the oldest known Thyreophora dinosaurs, *Scelidosaurus* was a small dino covered in rows of scales called scutes (similar to the scales on turtles and crocodiles). These would have been a defense against predators, and *Scelidosaurus* had scutes covering its neck, back, and tail. Paleontologists studied the length of its limbs and found that its back legs were longer than its front legs. That discovery led them to believe that *Scelidosaurus* could rear up on its hind legs; this motion would have helped it to reach vegetation that was higher up on trees.

NAME MEANING: Limb lizard
ERA IT LIVED IN: Early Jurassic Period of Europe
SIZE: 12.5 feet (3.8 meters) long and 595 pounds (269.9 kilograms)
DIET: Herbivorous

STEGOSAURUS

Stegosaurus plates are iconic in dinosaur imagery, but their actual purpose has been a subject of debate among paleontologists. When *Stegosaurus* was originally discovered, paleontologists mistakenly thought its bony plates laid flat along its back. They called it the "roofed lizard" because they though the plates were like the shingles on a roof. After finding a *Stegosaurus* skeleton that had been preserved in mud with the plates in their proper upright position, they realized that their first descriptions of this creature were incorrect.

The tall, broad plates along its back might have been for display, but some paleontologists think that they may have been used for thermoregulation (meaning they helped *Scelidosaurus* keep its body temperature in check). *Stegosaurus* had four spikes on its tail that might have been useful weapons against predators—cartoonist Gary Larson named these spikes thagomizers. *Stegosaurus* also had a form of defense on its neck, called gular armor, to protect it from predators.

NAME MEANING: Roof lizard
ERA IT LIVED IN: Late Jurassic Period of North America
SIZE: Up to 29.5 feet (9 meters) long and 7.7 tons (7 metric tons)
DIET: Herbivorous

TUOJIANGOSAURUS

Dinosaurs on different continents were sometimes related to one another, and that's exactly the case with *Tuojiangosaurus*. While *Stegosaurus* lived in North America, its relative *Tuojiangosaurus* was one of the first stegosaurid dinosaurs discovered in China. *Tuojiangosaurus* looked similar to *Stegosaurus*, but its plates were taller and narrower.

NAME MEANING: Tuo River lizard
ERA IT LIVED IN: Late Jurassic Period of Asia
SIZE: 21.3 feet (6.5 meters) long and 2.8 tons (2.5 metric tons)
DIET: Herbivorous

KENTROSAURUS

NAME MEANING: Sharp point lizard
ERA IT LIVED IN: Late Jurassic
Period of Africa
SIZE: 15 feet (4.6 meters) long
and 1.1 tons (1 metric ton)
DIET: Herbivorous

The biggest difference between *Kentrosaurus* and *Stegosaurus* was that *Kentrosaurus* had longer spikes on its tail, as well as spikes on its shoulders. *Kentrosaurus* was smaller than *Stegosaurus*, so the spikes would have been extra defense against larger predators.

MIRAGAIA

The long neck of *Miragaia* looks an awful lot like a sauropod's—it had 17 vertebrae in its elongated neck. But the plates and spikes running down its back made *Miragaia* undoubtedly part of the stegosaur family. The first fossils were found in Europe, but new evidence at the Morrison Formation has led paleontologists to believe *Miragaia* might have been in North America as well.

NAME MEANING: Wonderful Gaia
ERA IT LIVED IN: Late Jurassic Period of Europe and possibly North America
SIZE: 21 feet (6.4 meters) long and 2 tons (1.8 metric tons)
DIET: Herbivorous

BOREALOPELTA

Thyreophora dinosaurs were known for their unique armor, but *Borealopelta* took its defensive methods one step further. Paleontologists have found incredibly well-preserved *Borealopelta* (similar to mummies) that allowed them to study their skin pigment. *Borealopelta* would have had reddish-brown skin that could have acted as camouflage, helping it to blend into its surroundings and avoid being noticed by predators. If a predator did find it, though, *Borealopelta* still had plenty of defense, thanks to its scaly, armored skin and spikes.

Paleontologists also found unique material in the stomach of one of the "mummy" *Borealopelta*. The contents of its stomach were preserved, and paleontologists learned that it ate ferns and plant stems, but there was also evidence of wood and charcoal.

SAUROPELTA

Sauropelta was part of a group of dinosaurs called nodosaurids, a family within the ankylosaur group. The other family in the ankylosaur group was the ankylosaurids, and the main difference between ankylosaurids and nodosaurids was their tails. Ankylosaurids had "club" tails with spikes that made the tail look like a mace. Nodosaurids didn't have clubbed tails; rather, their tails were pointed at the tip.

Like other ankylosaurs, *Sauropelta* was quadrupedal, herbivorous, and armored. It had long spikes on its neck that projected out to the sides, and paleontologists have studied the tendons in its tail to determine that *Sauropelta* may have been able to swing its tail to strike approaching predators.

NAME MEANING: Lizard shield
ERA IT LIVED IN: Early Cretaceous Period of North America
SIZE: 17.1 feet (5.2 meters) long and 1.7 tons (1.5 metric tons)
DIET: Herbivorous

LIAONINGOSAURUS

A fossil specimen of *Liaoningosaurus* had fossil fish in its stomach that it would have caught using its long, sharp teeth. The fish were a very exciting find for paleontologists, because it means that *Liaoningosaurus* could have had a semiaquatic lifestyle (a first for the ankylosaurids).

NAME MEANING: Liaoning Province lizard
ERA IT LIVED IN: Early Cretaceous Period of Asia
SIZE: 1 foot (0.3 meters) long
DIET: Either carnivorous or omnivorous

ANKYLOSAURUS

Paleontologists haven't found a complete skeleton of *Ankylosaurus* yet (so far they have its skull, shoulders, upper arm, thigh, neck, tail club, and dermal armor). But because they've got fossils of different body parts of its relatives (like *Euoplocephalus* and *Tarchia*), they're able to guess at some of the missing pieces to determine what it would look like.

The most notable feature of *Ankylosaurus* is its osteoderms. The rounded, flat plates would have covered most of its body (excluding its belly), and they would have worked like a suit of armor to protect *Ankylosaurus*. The rounded spikes on its body would have provided even more protection, and its clubbed tail would have helped *Ankylosaurus* to fight off the large predators in its environment, like *Tyrannosaurus*.

NAME MEANING: Fused lizard
ERA IT LIVED IN: Late Cretaceous Period of North America
SIZE: Up to 26 feet (7.9 meters) long and 8 tons (7.3 metric tons)
DIET: Herbivorous

NAME MEANING: Well-armed head
ERA IT LIVED IN: Late Cretaceous Period of North America
SIZE: 18 feet (5.5 meters) long and 2.5 tons (2.3 metric tons)
DIET: Herbivorous

EUOPLOCEPHALUS

Paleontologists didn't just study what ankylosaurids looked like on the outside; they also looked at the cranial anatomy of *Euoplocephalus*. It had a looped nasal cavity that paleontologists think might have helped *Euoplocephalus* with vocal resonance (making loud sounds) or thermoregulation (controlling body temperature). They also studied how the jaw of *Euoplocephalus* would have moved and determined that it could move its jaw forward and sideways, which would have helped it to shear through tough vegetation.

TARCHIA

Fossils of *Tarchia* found in Asia were incredibly helpful for paleontologists studying ankylosaurids. Its skeleton was nearly complete, and included its skull, ribs, hip bones, osteoderms, vertebrae, and tail club. When other ankylosaurids have less complete fossil skeletons, paleontologists can refer to *Tarchia* to help fill in the blanks.

Studying the pelvis and tail of *Tarchia* revealed injuries on the bones, which tells paleontologists that *Tarchia* was probably injured in combat.

NAME MEANING: Brainy one
ERA IT LIVED IN: Late Cretaceous Period of Asia
SIZE: 18 feet (5.5 meters) long and 2.5 tons (2.3 metric tons)
DIET: Herbivorous

ZUUL

Who you gonna call? Paleontologists! *Zuul* was named after the spiky, dinosaur-like creature in *Ghostbusters* that looks a lot like this ankylosaurid. Fossils of *Zuul* (discovered in 2014) were the only complete set of remains found at the Judith River Formation in Montana. Its osteoderms, skin impressions, skull, and tail club were incredibly well preserved, which helped paleontologists to better understand its relatives *Ankylosaurus* and *Euoplocephalus*.

NAME MEANING: Named after the demon character from the 1984 film *Ghostbusters*

ERA IT LIVED IN: Late Cretaceous Period of North America

SIZE: 20 feet (6.1 meters) long and 2.5 tons (2.3 metric tons)

DIET: Herbivorous

EDMONTONIA

Edmontonia had large, forward-facing spikes along its neck, but—unlike ankylosaurids and nodosaurids—its tail didn't have any spikes on it. One specimen of *Edmontonia* with well-preserved osteoderms and skin impressions is on display at the American Museum of Natural History in New York City.

NAME MEANING: Named after the Edmonton Formation

ERA IT LIVED IN: Late Cretaceous Period of North America

SIZE: 22 feet (6.7 meters) long and 3 tons (2.7 metric tons)

DIET: Herbivorous

NEORNITHISCHIA

Like Thyreophora, Neornithischia dinosaurs are broken up into two main groups. The Ornithopoda ("bird-foot") dinosaurs were small, birdlike herbivores, including the hadrosaurs—commonly known as the "duck-bill" dinosaurs.

The other main group of Neornithischia was Marginocephalia ("fringed heads"). This group is again divided in two. Pachycephalosauria dinosaurs were bipedal and typically herbivores or omnivores, and most had a domed skull. Ceratopsia ("horned faces") dinosaurs were beaked herbivores that typically had large facial horns or frills.

DRYOSAURUS

Just like how doctors use CT scans to learn more about people, paleontologists can use CT scans on fossils to learn more about dinosaurs. By doing CT scans on the skulls of *Dryosaurus*, paleontologists learned how it changed as it aged. Their eye sockets got smaller, they gained more tooth positions, and their brain changed size as they developed. Have you ever heard the saying "the best defense is a good offense"? That's the strategy paleontologists think *Dryosaurus* would have taken. With its long legs it would have been quick and agile, making it easier to run away from predatory theropods in its environment.

NAME MEANING: Tree lizard
ERA IT LIVED IN: Late Jurassic Period of North America
SIZE: 14 feet (4.3 meters) long and 200 pounds (90.7 kilograms)
DIET: Herbivorous

NAME MEANING: Three-horned face

ERA IT LIVED IN: Late Cretaceous Period of North America

SIZE: Up to 29 feet (8.8 meters) long and 12 tons (10.9 metric tons)

DIET: Herbivorous

TRICERATOPS

Pop culture loves the *Triceratops*. This dinosaur is iconic with its large, bony frill and three-horned face. But have you ever wondered why it looks like this? Paleontologists have, and they've studied what the purpose of the frill and horns would have been. *Triceratops* was an herbivore that ate palm plants, cycads, and ferns, so it didn't use the horns for hunting, but it may have used them for defense.

Triceratops lived in the same environment as *Tyrannosaurus*, and paleontologists have found bite marks on *Triceratops* bones that likely came from *Tyrannosaurus*. The frill could have been a defense display to make *Triceratops* look bigger and scarier, but paleontologists also think that the frill could have been used for courtship or identification. Lots of modern animals have physical features that are meant to attract mates, so it makes sense for the frill to have been a courtship feature. Also, even dinosaurs needed to be able to distinguish one individual from another, which means it would be useful for *Triceratops* to have frills as a way to identify themselves.

IGUANODON

Paleontologists first started describing and classifying dinosaurs in the 1800s, and *Iguanodon* was one of the first to be described. At first, paleontologists thought that *Iguanodon* would have walked around on all fours, making it look like a giant lizard (like an iguana). The fossils also included what looked like a horn, and paleontologists assumed it would have been a nose horn (like a rhino).

But as they recovered more *Iguanodon* fossils, paleontologists realized that it looked very different from how they originally pictured this dinosaur. *Iguanodon* didn't walk quite like a lizard, and paleontologists now think that it may have been capable of both bipedal and quadrupedal walking. They also realized that the "horn" wasn't a horn at all; it was actually a spike that sat on *Iguanodon*'s hands like a thumb. The thumb spike wouldn't have moved like a finger, but it might have served as a defense against predators.

NAME MEANING: Iguana tooth
ERA IT LIVED IN: Early Cretaceous Period of Europe
SIZE: 30 feet (9.1 meters) long and 3.4 tons (3.1 metric tons); some specimens would have reached lengths of 43 feet (13.1 meters).
DIET: Herbivorous

PSITTACOSAURUS

Have you ever wondered about dinosaur digestion? *Psittacosaurus* fossils gave paleontologists some insight. It was an herbivore with a robust beak and prominent cheekbones, and paleontologists have found preserved gastroliths in *Psittacosaurus* fossils. Gastroliths are stomach stones, which would have helped *Psittacosaurus* to grind down all the plant material it ate.

NAME MEANING: Parrot lizard
ERA IT LIVED IN: Early Cretaceous Period of Asia
SIZE: Up to 6 feet (1.8 meters) long and over 44 pounds (20 kilograms)
DIET: Herbivorous

TENONTOSAURUS

There are lots of fossil sites across the United States, and *Tenontosaurus* has been found in a handful of different states, including Montana, Wyoming, Oklahoma, Texas, Idaho, Utah, and Maryland. Some fossils of *Tenontosaurus* have been found in the same place as *Deinonychus*, which usually hints to paleontologists that the two dinosaurs had a prey-predator relationship. But adult *Tenontosaurus* would have been bigger than *Deinonychus*, making them unlikely prey. Instead, paleontologists think that *Deinonychus* would have hunted juvenile *Tenontosaurus*, which grew at a slower pace than other ornithopods.

NAME MEANING: Sinew lizard
ERA IT LIVED IN: Early Cretaceous Period of North America
SIZE: 26 feet (7.9 meters) long and 2 tons (1.8 metric tons)
DIET: Herbivorous

LEPTOCERATOPS

Leptoceratops was a small dinosaur compared to other herbivores sharing its environment (like *Triceratops*). Because of its size, it would have been better adapted to eating low-growing plants (instead of the higher vegetation *Triceratops* could reach). By studying its lower jaws and teeth, paleontologists have learned that *Leptoceratops* would have been able to chew through tough plant material.

NAME MEANING: Thin-horned face
ERA IT LIVED IN: Late Cretaceous Period of North America
SIZE: 6.6 feet (2 meters) long and 441 pounds (200 kilograms)
DIET: Herbivorous

ZUNICERATOPS

The ceratopsian dinosaurs were a group of beaked herbivore dinosaurs within the Neornithischia family that included smaller dinosaurs like *Psittacosaurus* along with horned dinosaurs like *Zuniceratops*. The *Zuniceratops* had horns over its eyes, a unique feature for early ceratopsian dinosaurs, but it paved the way for the lineage of dinosaurs called ceratopsids (the horned and frilled "ceratops" dinosaurs like *Triceratops*).

NAME MEANING: Zuni-horned face
ERA IT LIVED IN: Late Cretaceous Period of North America
SIZE: 7.2 feet (2.2 meters) long and 386 pounds (175.1 kilograms)
DIET: Herbivorous

TOROSAURUS

When paleontologists first encountered *Torosaurus*, they thought that it might be an older version of *Triceratops*, but the two had a few different features. *Torosaurus* had a longer skull and shorter nose horn than *Triceratops*, and it also had holes (or perforations) in its frill that *Triceratops* didn't have. A fossil find in Canada in 2022 shed even more light on *Torosaurus*. Two specimens were found that were identified as juveniles, which showed that young *Torosaurus* was indeed different from young *Triceratops*.

NAME MEANING: Perforated lizard

ERA IT LIVED IN: Late Cretaceous Period of North America

SIZE: 30 feet (9.1 meters) long and 7 tons (6.4 metric tons)

DIET: Herbivorous

STYRACOSAURUS

The spiky *Styracosaurus* was the star of a 2020 study where paleontologists analyzed their horns and frills. In juveniles, the frills were short and the spikes on their neck were nubs. But as they grew, the frills and spikes got larger. The horns on *Styracosaurus* would have been slightly different on each individual, and they weren't always symmetrical. Marks from *Styracosaurus* horns have been found on the skulls of other dinosaurs that shared their environment, so it's possible that *Styracosaurus* was combative.

PACHYRHINOSAURUS

The large, bony mass that *Pachyrhinosaurus* had over its nose looks a little different from other ceratopsids; the mass is called a boss, and *Pachyrhinosaurus* may have used its horned head to ram or shove (like bighorn sheep and musk oxen).

NAME MEANING: Thick-nosed lizard
ERA IT LIVED IN: Late Cretaceous Period of North America
SIZE: 26 feet (7.9 meters) long and 3.3 tons (3 metric tons)
DIET: Herbivorous

CENTROSAURUS

Predators weren't the only threat to dinosaurs. The environment they lived in could be dangerous, and even large dinosaurs were susceptible to natural disasters. One bone bed in Canada showed a herd of *Centrosaurus* that was killed by a storm surge or hurricane. And, just like modern animals, dinosaurs were vulnerable to health issues. One well-preserved *Centrosaurus* from the Canadian bone bed was studied in 2020, and paleontologists could see evidence of bone cancer on its leg.

NAME MEANING: Pointed lizard
ERA IT LIVED IN: Late Cretaceous Period of North America
SIZE: Up to 18 feet (4.8 meters) long
DIET: Herbivorous

NASUTOCERATOPS

Nasutoceratops was unique compared to other ceratopsids because of its brow and nose horns. Its nose horns were bulbous, and its curved brow horns looked like modern cattle's. It was one of the first ceratopsids to be found in the American Southwest (most other ceratopsids were found in the northern states of the U.S. and Canada).

NAME MEANING: Large nosed-horned face

ERA IT LIVED IN: Late Cretaceous Period of North America

SIZE: 14.8 feet (4.5 meters) long and 1.5 tons (1.4 metric tons)

DIET: Herbivorous

PACHYCEPHALOSAURUS

The skull of *Pachycephalosaurus* told paleontologists a lot about how it behaved. It had a rounded dome on its head and spikes behind its skull, and it would have headbutted like a bighorn sheep. The skull also told paleontologists about its growth. Young *Pachycephalosaurus* had a flat head and prominent spikes, but as it got older its head became rounder and more domed, and its spikes shortened into bumps.

NAME MEANING: Thick-headed lizard
ERA IT LIVED IN: Late Cretaceous Period of North America
SIZE: 14.8 feet (4.5 meters) long and 990 pounds (449.1 kilograms)
DIET: Omnivorous

PROTOCERATOPS

Protoceratops was an early member of the ceratopsian family, so it looked a little different from later ceratopsian dinosaurs. It didn't have large brow or nose horns (like *Triceratops*), but it did have a telltale ceratopsian neck frill. Its frill was unique because it had large holes in it, called fenestrae, that made the frill lighter.

NAME MEANING: First-horned face

ERA IT LIVED IN: Late Cretaceous Period of Asia

SIZE: Up to 5.9 feet (1.8 meters) long and 182 pounds (82.6 kilograms)

DIET: Herbivorous

BRACHYLOPHOSAURUS

One *Brachylophosaurus* specimen was more of a mummy than a fossil—it was preserved with remnants of tissue and tendons, which gave paleontologists incredible insight into what this dinosaur would have looked like in real life. The mummy *Brachylophosaurus* was nicknamed "Leonardo," and he wasn't the only well-preserved *Brachylophosaurus*. Paleontologists have also studied *Brachylophosaurus* with preserved tumors and preserved plant material in their stomach.

NAME MEANING: Short-crested lizard
ERA IT LIVED IN: Late Cretaceous Period of North America
SIZE: Up to 36 feet (11 meters) long and 7.7 tons (7 metric tons)
DIET: Herbivorous

EDMONTOSAURUS

If you live in the U.S., you could see a dinosaur "mummy" for yourself if you take a trip to New York. Paleontologists have observed soft tissue called a hoof pad, skin impressions, crests, and tendons on *Edmontosaurus* because there are so many well-preserved specimens. One of these mummies is on display at the American Museum of Natural History in New York City.

NAME MEANING: Edmonton lizard
ERA IT LIVED IN: Late Cretaceous Period of North America
SIZE: Up to 39 feet (11.9 meters) long and 4.4 tons (4 metric tons). Larger specimens may have reached sizes of up to 49 feet (14.9 meters) long and 10 tons (9.1 metric tons).
DIET: Herbivorous

PARASAUROLOPHUS

Some dinosaurs have unique features called crests, and *Parasaurolophus* is one of them. The crest on *Parasaurolophus* has been studied by paleontologists and at first they thought the crests differed between males and females. But as they studied more fossils of *Parasaurolophus*, they discovered that the crest was less about gender and more about age; the crest got bigger as *Parasaurolophus* grew.

The crest also had complex airways and nasal passages, and paleontologists think it might have been a resonance chamber. Resonance chambers transfer sound into the air, and paleontologists think that *Parasaurolophus* would have made deep, low-pitched sounds.

NAME MEANING: Near crested lizard

ERA IT LIVED IN: Late Cretaceous Period of North America

SIZE: Up to 31 feet (9.4 meters) long and 2.5 tons (2.3 metric tons)

DIET: Herbivorous

CORYTHOSAURUS

Like *Parasaurolophus*, *Corythosaurus* was a dinosaur with a crest, and it's a very interesting feature for paleontologists to study. The exact function of the crest is debated among paleontologists. When it was first studied, paleontologists thought the crest would work like a snorkel, allowing *Corythosaurus* to breathe and swim. But the crest didn't have any kind of airflow opening to support that theory, so they kept studying. It could have been just a display that helped *Corythosaurus* find a mate, and it may have been a feature that grew as *Corythosaurus* aged. One of the most interesting theories paleontologists have come up with is that the crest was a way to communicate. *Corythosaurus* might have been able to make a low-pitched sound with its crest that would help it communicate with the rest of its herd.

Corythosaurus was part of a family of dinosaurs called hadrosaurids, and it's one of several hadrosaurids to be found with preserved skin impressions.

NAME MEANING: Helmet lizard

ERA IT LIVED IN: Late Cretaceous Period of North America

SIZE: 30 feet (9.1 meters) long and 3.8 tons (3.4 metric tons)

DIET: Herbivorous

MAIASAURA

Maiasaura was a groundbreaking paleontological find that helped paleontologists better understand dinosaur behaviors. Fossils of *Maiasaura* were first discovered next to young *Maiasaura* and a nest of *Maiasaura* eggs. This Montana site was nicknamed Egg Mountain, and it was important because it showed that dinosaurs likely took care of their young—that's how *Maiasaura* got the name "good mother."

Maiasaura fossils also told paleontologists a lot about dinosaur ages and growth. Most of the fossils were young, but by studying them they were able to learn that juveniles had a higher mortality rate than adults. That means that lots of *Maiasaura* died when they were younger. Why is that? Younger *Maiasaura* would have been smaller. They didn't reach their full adult size until they were about 8 years old. And because they were smaller, they would have been more likely targets for predators. If *Maiasaura* survived to adulthood, paleontologists think that it changed from being bipedal to quadrupedal.

NAME MEANING LIZARD: Good mother lizard
ERA IT LIVED IN: Late Cretaceous Period of North America
SIZE: Up to 30 feet (9.1 meters) long
DIET: Herbivorous

OTHER FOSSIL FINDS

Paleontologists study a lot more than just dinosaurs. And that's because there are a lot more fossils out there than just dinosaurs. Fossils can also include ancient plants, coral, and petrified wood; insects, bugs, and parasites; aquatic invertebrates, crustaceans, bivalves, fish, whales, and sharks; and mammals like ancient elephants, horses, canines, and felines. There are even fossils of people (and the ancestors of humans) that teach paleontologists about evolution.

In this section we're going to look at just a few non-dinosaur fossil finds of some interesting ancient animals. But there are a LOT more fossils out there—keep researching and learning about all different kinds!

PTERODACTYL

Winged, flying reptiles called pterosaurs might look like modern birds, but they actually aren't related (birds descended from the theropods). *Pterodactyl* fossils were first discovered in 1784, and paleontologists originally thought that its wings were paddles and that the *Pterodactyl* lived in the water. But by 1801 paleontologists had learned that *Pterodactyl* could fly using the wings, which stretched over its elongated fingers.

NAME MEANING: Winged finger
ERA IT LIVED IN: Cretaceous and Jurassic Periods
SIZE: Wingspan of about 3.5 feet (1.1 meters)
DIET: Carnivorous

EOHIPPUS

Eohippus is considered by paleontologists to be one of the first horses to walk the Earth. It had long, deerlike limbs and would have been able to run quickly to avoid predators. It wasn't nearly as big as the modern horse. Paleontologists think it would have weighed around 50 pounds (22.7 kilograms), making it closer to the size of a dog than a horse. Studying its teeth revealed to paleontologists that, unlike its modern horse relatives, *Eohippus* wouldn't have eaten grass—it likely grazed on low-hanging leaves.

NAME MEANING: Dawn horse
ERA IT LIVED IN: Cenozoic Era
SIZE: About 2 feet (0.6 meters) tall
DIET: Herbivorous

PALAEOLOXODON

Paleontologists think *Palaeoloxodon* may have been one of the largest mammals to ever walk the Earth. It was part of a group of mammals called *Proboscidea*, and it was related to the mammoth and modern-day elephant (including the genus *Loxodonta*). Fossils of *Palaeoloxodon* found across Asia include its two long, straight tusks. Even its individual bones were enormous. One thigh bone found in India in 1905 measured more than 5 feet (1.5 meters) long.

NAME MEANING: Before Loxodon
ERA IT LIVED IN: Cenozoic Era
SIZE: Up to 16 feet (4.9 meters) tall and 24 tons (21.8 metric tons)
DIET: Herbivorous

ARCHAEOTHERIUM

This prehistoric piglike creature was first discovered in 1850 in North America. By studying its skull, paleontologists have learned that it would have had forward-facing eyes with good vision, a keen sense of smell for hunting, and jaws with large canine teeth that could open wide and easily close around prey.

NAME MEANING: Ancient beast
ERA IT LIVED IN: Cenozoic Era
SIZE: About 7 feet (2.1 meters) long
DIET: Carnivorous

SMILODON

You might know this creature by its more common name: the saber-toothed tiger. Its long, slender canine teeth, which look like saber swords, are fascinating to both paleontologists and prehistoric animal lovers. It would have had a tigerlike body and a short tail like a bobcat, but despite its physical appearance, it wasn't related to modern big cats (their ancestors didn't appear until a few million years later).

NAME MEANING: Scalpel tooth
ERA IT LIVED IN: Cenozoic Era
SIZE: About 7.5 feet (2.3 meters) long
DIET: Carnivorous

ATRACTOSTEUS

Atractosteus was part of an alligator-like family of creatures known as gar, which has a special type of organ called a "swim bladder" that functions like lungs. Paleontologists know a great deal about what *Atractosteus* looked like because of exquisitely preserved fossils from prehistoric lakes that include the scales still in place. Although they were slow-moving at times, these carnivores could move quickly when they were on the hunt for prey like fish and crustaceans.

NAME MEANING: Arrow bone
ERA IT LIVED IN: Cenozoic Era
SIZE: Up to 7 feet (2.1 meters) long
DIET: Carnivorous

DORUDON

The evolution of whales has long been a fascinating subject for paleontologists. About 55 million years ago, land-based ancestors of whales began to walk into the ocean. They started out as hoofed mammals that swam in lakes and rivers and, over time, they became increasingly adapted to life in the water. By about 40 million years ago, the walking whales had given rise to ones that lived their whole lives in the sea. *Dorudon* was part of the evolutionary process from walking to swimming. The legs sticking out from the sides of *Dorudon* connect them to their amphibious ancestors, but they likely weren't very useful for walking or moving on land.

Dorudon were predators in the sea, and paleontologists have found fossilized stomach contents showing that the last thing this prehistoric whale fed on was fish. Because of its teeth and jaw shape, paleontologists speculate that it may have also eaten some small marine mammals. *Dorudon* would have had a long, narrow snout. Modern beaked whales have a similar snout shape, but *Dorudon* wouldn't have had a large "melon." Modern whales have a bulging area of their head called a melon that's often important for echolocation.

Dorudon fossils come from an area in Egypt called the Tethys Sea, which was an ancient body of water that used to connect the Mediterranean Sea and the Indian Ocean but is now land. This area is known as the "Valley of the Whales," because fossils from whale ancestors have been found there.

NAME MEANING: Spear tooth
ERA IT LIVED IN: Cenozoic Era
SIZE: About 16 feet (4.9 meters) long
DIET: Carnivorous

NAME MEANING: Giant tooth
ERA IT LIVED IN: Cenozoic Era
SIZE: Up to 52 feet (15.8 meters) long
and 65 tons (59 metric tons)
DIET: Carnivorous

MEGALODON

Of all the sharks to ever swim the seas, *Megalodon* was the biggest. *Megalodon*'s serrated teeth had a triangular shape similar to that of a modern white shark, but they were significantly larger. A white shark's tooth is usually about 2 inches (5.1 centimeters) long, but *Megalodon* had teeth that were nearly 7 inches (17.8 centimeters) long. From tooth marks on bones, paleontologists know that *Megalodon* frequently fed on blubbery whales.

Megalodon roamed the seas for nearly 14 million years. Its fossils have been found on every continent except Antarctica. Though they seem to have preferred warmer waters, paleontologists think that *Megalodon* may have had a specialized way of regulating its temperature that's similar to that of the white shark, which is not exclusively warm blooded. This would have allowed *Megalodon* to swim in colder water that other predators couldn't access, putting it at the top of the food chain.

ABOUT CIDER MILL PRESS BOOK PUBLISHERS

Good ideas ripen with time. From seed to harvest, Cider Mill Press
brings fine reading, information, and entertainment together between
the covers of its creatively crafted books. Our Cider Mill bears fruit
twice a year, publishing a new crop of titles each spring and fall.

"Where good books are ready for press"
501 Nelson Place
Nashville, Tennessee 37214

cidermillpress.com